PAT

Patrol Name

Patrol Symbol

Created by Clarke Green
Scoutmastercg.com
First Published in 2013

How to Use This Logbook

Keeping a record of meetings, camping trips plans, adventures and memorable moments is a great way to become a better patrol.

Reviewing the information in your patrol log will help your patrol understand what they should start doing, keep on doing or, perhaps, stop doing.

Your logbook should, of course relate all the fun, adventure and friendship your patrol shares. Be sure to write down all of your achievements and successes, but don't forget to include your flops and failures.

By reflecting on both successes, things that don't go as planned, and things that just didn't work you can avoid past mistakes and make better plans for the next time.

Include a description of the places you visit, what you see there and the conditions you encounter (like the weather).

The logbook is divided into sections that will help keep your records organized – here's how to use each of them:

Patrol Roster

Keep a roster of your patrol members and other important leaders from your troop. Be sure to include contact information.

Table of Contents

To keep track of your records be sure to record meeting dates, notes and locations in the table of contents.

Meetings

Use these pages to track your planning and to keep everyone up to date. There's space for recording who attends the meeting, a checklist where you can record the tasks that need to be accomplished at the meeting, the plans you make, and who will be responsible for carrying them out (there's also plenty of space to keep additional notes of discussions and decisions).

Camping Trips

There's room in this logbook to record a baker's dozen (13) short-term camping trips (one or two nights) and three long-term trips (three to seven nights).

Keep a record of who attends the trip, what you may try to do different next time, and note if you forgot to pack something or if a piece of gear needs to be repaired.

Each trip record includes a section titled 'roses and thorns'. To use the rose, thorn, and bud idea; every Scout shares three things;

1. A rose is something good that happened.

2. A thorn is a challenge they encountered

3. A bud is something you'd like to do in the future.

Here's an example of a rose, thorn and bud from one patrol member:

NAME	SHORT-TERM CAMPING TRIP 1 **ROSES, THORNS and BUDS**
John S.	Swimming was great, I did a backflip!
	We had to get up really early.
	I hope we can do more swimming tomorrow!

Short-term camping records have one 'rose and thorn' page for the whole trip and two pages for additional notes. Long-term camping records have daily 'rose and thorn' pages and a page for additional notes each day.

General Notes

There are plenty of blank pages for additional notes. There's a place to title each page, and you can keep track of them by writing that title and page number in the table of contents.

Progress or Record Charts

There are a number of progress or record charts you can use to track attendance, rank advancement or anything you like.

TABLE OF CONTENTS

Meeting Records

Date			Notes	Record	Page
				Meeting Record 1	2
				Meeting Record 2	4
				Meeting Record 3	6
				Meeting Record 4	8
				Meeting Record 5	10
				Meeting Record 6	12
				Meeting Record 7	14
				Meeting Record 8	16
				Meeting Record 9	18
				Meeting Record 10	20
				Meeting Record 11	22
				Meeting Record 12	24
				Meeting Record 13	26
				Meeting Record 14	28
				Meeting Record 15	30
				Meeting Record 16	32
				Meeting Record 17	34
				Meeting Record 18	36
				Meeting Record 19	38
				Meeting Record 20	40

				Record	Page
				Meeting Record 21	42
				Meeting Record 22	44
				Meeting Record 23	46
				Meeting Record 24	48
				Meeting Record 25	50
				Meeting Record 26	52
				Meeting Record 27	54
				Meeting Record 28	56
				Meeting Record 29	58
				Meeting Record 30	60
				Meeting Record 31	62
				Meeting Record 32	64
				Meeting Record 33	66
				Meeting Record 34	68
				Meeting Record 35	70
				Meeting Record 36	72
				Meeting Record 37	74
				Meeting Record 38	76
				Meeting Record 39	78
				Meeting Record 40	80

Short -Term Camping Records

Date			Location	Record	Page
				Short-Term Camp 1	84
				Short-Term Camp 2	88
				Short-Term Camp 3	92

Date	Location			Record	Page
				Short-Term Camp 4	96
				Short-Term Camp 5	100
				Short-Term Camp 6	104
				Short-Term Camp 7	108
				Short-Term Camp 8	112
				Short-Term Camp 9	116
				Short-Term Camp 10	120
				Short-Term Camp 11	124
				Short-Term Camp 12	128
				Short-Term Camp 13	132

Long-Term Camping Records

Date	Location			Record	Page
				Long-Term Camp 1	138
				Long-Term Camp 2	154
				Long-Term Camp 3	170

General Patrol Notes and Progress Charts

Title	Page

PATROL ROSTER

Name	Patrol Job	Phone
1	Patrol Leader	
2	Assistant Patrol Leader	
3	Patrol Scribe	
4	Patrol Quartermaster	
5		
6		
7		
8		

Troop Leaders	Name	Phone
Senior Patrol Leader		
Scoutmaster		

PATROL MEETING NOTES

MEETING 1

Attending

Date [ ][ ][ ]

1

5

2

6

3

7

4

8

What needs to be done

☐

☐

☐

☐

☐

☐

☐

Plans and decisions

Person Responsible

MEETING 1 ADDITIONAL NOTES

MEETING 2

Date

Attending

1

2

3

4

5

6

7

8

What needs to be done

☐

☐

☐

☐

☐

☐

☐

Plans and decisions   Person Responsible

4

MEETING 2 ADDITIONAL NOTES

MEETING 3

Attending

Date

1

2

3

4

5

6

7

8

What needs to be done

☐

☐

☐

☐

☐

☐

☐

Plans and decisions

Person Responsible

MEETING 3 ADDITIONAL NOTES

MEETING 4

Attending

Date [ ][ ][ ]

1

5

2

6

3

7

4

8

What needs to be done

- [ ]
- [ ]
- [ ]
- [ ]
- [ ]
- [ ]
- [ ]

Plans and decisions

Person Responsible

MEETING 5

Attending

Date

1

2

3

4

5

6

7

8

What needs to be done

☐

☐

☐

☐

☐

☐

☐

Plans and decisions

Person Responsible

MEETING 5 ADDITIONAL NOTES

MEETING 6

Attending

Date

1

2

3

4

5

6

7

8

What needs to be done

- [ ]
- [ ]
- [ ]
- [ ]
- [ ]
- [ ]
- [ ]

Plans and decisions   Person Responsible

MEETING 7

Attending

Date

1 ....

2 ....

3 ....

4 ....

5 ....

6 ....

7 ....

8 ....

What needs to be done

☐ ....

☐ ....

☐ ....

☐ ....

☐ ....

☐ ....

☐

Plans and decisions   **Person Responsible**

14

MEETING 7 ADDITIONAL NOTES

MEETING 8

Date

Attending

1   5

2   6

3   7

4   8

What needs to be done

- [ ]
- [ ]
- [ ]
- [ ]
- [ ]
- [ ]
- [ ]

Plans and decisions   Person Responsible

MEETING 8 ADDITIONAL NOTES

MEETING 9

Attending   **Date**

1 _____   5 _____

2 _____   6 _____

3 _____   7 _____

4 _____   8 _____

What needs to be done

☐ _____

☐ _____

☐ _____

☐ _____

☐ _____

☐ _____

☐ _____

Plans and decisions   **Person Responsible**

_____   _____

_____   _____

_____   _____

_____   _____

_____   _____

_____   _____

_____   _____

_____   _____

MEETING 9 ADDITIONAL NOTES

MEETING 10

Attending

Date

1 _____   5 _____

2 _____   6 _____

3 _____   7 _____

4 _____   8 _____

What needs to be done

☐ _____

☐ _____

☐ _____

☐ _____

☐ _____

☐ _____

☐ _____

Plans and decisions   **Person Responsible**

MEETING 11

Attending

Date

1

5

2

6

3

7

4

8

What needs to be done

☐

☐

☐

☐

☐

☐

☐

Plans and decisions	Person Responsible

MEETING 11 ADDITIONAL NOTES

MEETING 12

Attending

Date

1 _____

2 _____

3 _____

4 _____

5 _____

6 _____

7 _____

8 _____

What needs to be done

☐ _____

☐ _____

☐ _____

☐ _____

☐ _____

☐ _____

☐ _____

Plans and decisions   Person Responsible

MEETING 12 ADDITIONAL NOTES

MEETING 13

Attending   Date

1   5

2   6

3   7

4   8

What needs to be done

☐

☐

☐

☐

☐

☐

☐

Plans and decisions   Person Responsible

MEETING 13 ADDITIONAL NOTES

MEETING 14

Attending   Date

1 _____   5 _____

2 _____   6 _____

3 _____   7 _____

4 _____   8 _____

What needs to be done

☐ _____

☐ _____

☐ _____

☐ _____

☐ _____

☐ _____

☐ _____

Plans and decisions   Person Responsible

_____   _____

_____   _____

_____   _____

_____   _____

_____   _____

_____   _____

_____   _____

_____   _____

MEETING 15

Attending   Date

1   5

2   6

3   7

4   8

What needs to be done

- [ ]
- [ ]
- [ ]
- [ ]
- [ ]
- [ ]
- [ ]

Plans and decisions   **Person Responsible**

MEETING 16

Attending

Date

1

2

3

4

5

6

7

8

What needs to be done

☐

☐

☐

☐

☐

☐

☐

Plans and decisions

Person Responsible

MEETING 17

Attending

Date

1 _____   5 _____

2 _____   6 _____

3 _____   7 _____

4 _____   8 _____

What needs to be done

☐ _____

☐ _____

☐ _____

☐ _____

☐ _____

☐ _____

☐ _____

Plans and decisions

Person Responsible

34

MEETING 17 ADDITIONAL NOTES

MEETING 18

Attending

Date

1 _____ 5 _____

2 _____ 6 _____

3 _____ 7 _____

4 _____ 8 _____

What needs to be done

☐ _____

☐ _____

☐ _____

☐ _____

☐ _____

☐ _____

☐ _____

Plans and decisions

Person Responsible

MEETING 19

Attending
                                    Date

1   5

2   6

3   7

4   8

What needs to be done

☐

☐

☐

☐

☐

☐

☐

Plans and decisions   **Person Responsible**

MEETING 20

Attending

Date

1

5

2

6

3

7

4

8

What needs to be done

☐

☐

☐

☐

☐

☐

☐

Plans and decisions

Person Responsible

40

MEETING 20 ADDITIONAL NOTES

MEETING 21

Date

Attending

1

5

2

6

3

7

4

8

What needs to be done

☐

☐

☐

☐

☐

☐

☐

Plans and decisions

Person Responsible

MEETING 22

Attending

Date | | | |
---|---|---

1   5

2   6

3   7

4   8

What needs to be done

- [ ]
- [ ]
- [ ]
- [ ]
- [ ]
- [ ]
- [ ]

Plans and decisions   **Person Responsible**

MEETING 22 ADDITIONAL NOTES

MEETING 23

Attending   Date

1   5

2   6

3   7

4   8

What needs to be done

☐

☐

☐

☐

☐

☐

☐

Plans and decisions   Person Responsible

MEETING 23 ADDITIONAL NOTES

MEETING 24

Attending

1

2

3

4

5

6

7

8

What needs to be done

☐

☐

☐

☐

☐

☐

☐

Plans and decisions   Person Responsible

48

MEETING 25

Attending

Date

1

5

2

6

3

7

4

8

What needs to be done

☐

☐

☐

☐

☐

☐

☐

Plans and decisions

Person Responsible

50

MEETING 26

Attending

Date

1 ....

2 ....

3 ....

4 ....

5 ....

6 ....

7 ....

8 ....

What needs to be done

☐ ....

☐ ....

☐ ....

☐ ....

☐ ....

☐ ....

☐

Plans and decisions   Person Responsible

52

MEETING 27

Attending
Date

1 _____   5 _____

2 _____   6 _____

3 _____   7 _____

4 _____   8 _____

What needs to be done

☐ _____

☐ _____

☐ _____

☐ _____

☐ _____

☐ _____

☐ _____

Plans and decisions   Person Responsible

_____   _____

_____   _____

_____   _____

_____   _____

_____   _____

_____   _____

_____   _____

_____   _____

_____   _____

MEETING 27 ADDITIONAL NOTES

MEETING 28

Attending

Date

1

2

3

4

5

6

7

8

What needs to be done

☐

☐

☐

☐

☐

☐

☐

Plans and decisions

Person Responsible

MEETING 29

Date

Attending

1   5

2   6

3   7

4   8

What needs to be done

- [ ]
- [ ]
- [ ]
- [ ]
- [ ]
- [ ]
- [ ]

Plans and decisions   Person Responsible

MEETING 30

Attending

Date

1

2

3

4

5

6

7

8

What needs to be done

☐

☐

☐

☐

☐

☐

☐

Plans and decisions

Person Responsible

60

MEETING 31

Attending　　　　　　　　　　　**Date**

1   5

2   6

3   7

4   8

What needs to be done

☐

☐

☐

☐

☐

☐

☐

Plans and decisions　　　　　　　**Person Responsible**

MEETING 32

Attending   Date

1   5

2   6

3   7

4   8

What needs to be done

☐

☐

☐

☐

☐

☐

☐

Plans and decisions   Person Responsible

64

MEETING 32 ADDITIONAL NOTES

MEETING 33

Attending   Date

1   5

2   6

3   7

4   8

What needs to be done

☐

☐

☐

☐

☐

☐

☐

Plans and decisions   Person Responsible

66

MEETING 33 ADDITIONAL NOTES

MEETING 34

Attending

Date

1 _____   5 _____

2 _____   6 _____

3 _____   7 _____

4 _____   8 _____

What needs to be done

- [ ] _____
- [ ] _____
- [ ] _____
- [ ] _____
- [ ] _____
- [ ] _____
- [ ] _____

Plans and decisions	Person Responsible

MEETING 35

Attending

Date

1

2

3

4

5

6

7

8

What needs to be done

☐

☐

☐

☐

☐

☐

☐

Plans and decisions

Person Responsible

MEETING 36

Attending

Date

1

2

3

4

5

6

7

8

What needs to be done

☐
☐
☐
☐
☐
☐
☐

Plans and decisions

Person Responsible

MEETING 37

Attending   Date

1   5

2   6

3   7

4   8

What needs to be done

☐

☐

☐

☐

☐

☐

☐

Plans and decisions   Person Responsible

MEETING 38

Attending

Date

1

2

3

4

5

6

7

8

What needs to be done

☐

☐

☐

☐

☐

☐

☐

Plans and decisions

Person Responsible

MEETING 39

Attending

Date

1

5

2

6

3

7

4

8

What needs to be done

☐

☐

☐

☐

☐

☐

☐

Plans and decisions

Person Responsible

MEETING 40

Attending

Date

1 _____ 5 _____

2 _____ 6 _____

3 _____ 7 _____

4 _____ 8 _____

What needs to be done

☐ _____

☐ _____

☐ _____

☐ _____

☐ _____

☐ _____

☐ _____

Plans and decisions   **Person Responsible**

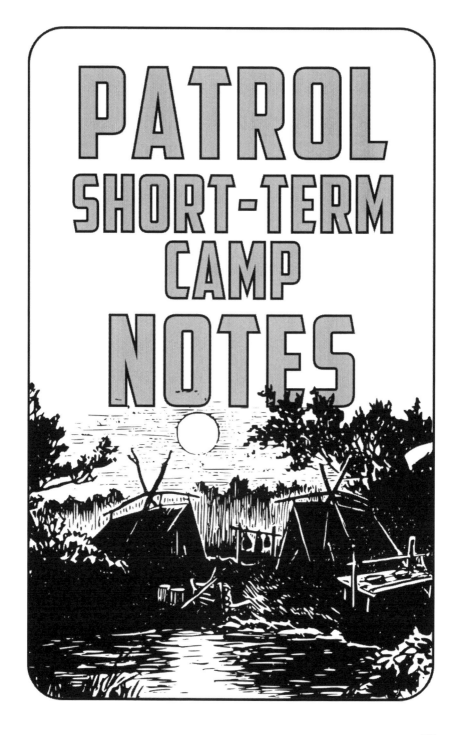

SHORT-TERM CAMPING TRIP 1

DATES: from ☐☐☐ to ☐☐☐

Location

Attending

1	5
2	6
3	7
4	8

Things to do differently

Gear repairs needed, things to bring next time:

SHORT-TERM CAMPING TRIP 2

DATES: from ⬚⬚⬚ to ⬚⬚⬚

Location

Attending

1
5

2
6

3
7

4
8

Things to do differently

Gear repairs needed, things to bring next time:

SHORT-TERM CAMPING TRIP 2 **ROSES, THORNS and BUDS**

SHORT-TERM CAMPING TRIP 3

DATES: from [ ] [ ] [ ] to [ ] [ ] [ ]

Location

Attending

1
2
3
4

5
6
7
8

Things to do differently

Gear repairs needed, things to bring next time:

SHORT-TERM CAMPING TRIP 4

DATES: from ⬚⬚⬚ to ⬚⬚⬚

Location

Attending

1

2

3

4

5

6

7

8

Things to do differently

Gear repairs needed, things to bring next time:

SHORT-TERM CAMPING TRIP 5

DATES: from [ ] [ ] [ ] to [ ] [ ] [ ]

Location

Attending

1   5

2   6

3   7

4   8

Things to do differently

Gear repairs needed, things to bring next time:

SHORT-TERM CAMPING TRIP 6

DATES: from ☐☐☐ to ☐☐☐

Location
....

Attending

1 ....   5 ....

2 ....   6 ....

3 ....   7 ....

4 ....   8 ....

Things to do differently

....

....

....

....

....

....

....

Gear repairs needed, things to bring next time:

....

....

....

....

....

....

SHORT-TERM CAMPING TRIP 7

DATES: from [ ][ ][ ] to [ ][ ][ ]

Location

Attending

1

2

3

4

5

6

7

8

Things to do differently

Gear repairs needed, things to bring next time:

SHORT-TERM CAMPING TRIP 8

DATES: from [   ] to [   ]

Location

Attending

1
5

2
6

3
7

4
8

Things to do differently

Gear repairs needed, things to bring next time:

SHORT-TERM CAMPING TRIP 9

DATES: from [ ][ ][ ] to [ ][ ][ ]

Location

Attending

1

2

3

4

5

6

7

8

Things to do differently

Gear repairs needed, things to bring next time:

SHORT-TERM CAMPING TRIP 10

DATES: from [ ][ ][ ] to [ ][ ][ ]

Location

Attending

1

2

3

4

5

6

7

8

Things to do differently

Gear repairs needed, things to bring next time:

SHORT-TERM CAMPING TRIP 11

DATES: from [   ][   ][   ] to [   ][   ][   ]

Location

Attending

1

2

3

4

5

6

7

8

Things to do differently

Gear repairs needed, things to bring next time:

SHORT-TERM CAMPING TRIP 12

DATES: from [ ][ ][ ] to [ ][ ][ ]

Location

Attending

1

2

3

4

5

6

7

8

Things to do differently

Gear repairs needed, things to bring next time:

SHORT-TERM CAMPING TRIP 13

DATES: from [   ][   ][   ] to [   ][   ][   ]

Location

Attending

1

2

3

4

5

6

7

8

Things to do differently

Gear repairs needed, things to bring next time:

PATROL
LONG-TERM
CAMP
NOTES

LONG-TERM CAMPING TRIP 1

DATES: from [ ][ ][ ] to [ ][ ][ ]

Location
....

Attending

1 ....

2 ....

3 ....

4 ....

5 ....

6 ....

7 ....

8 ....

Things to do differently

....

....

....

....

....

....

....

Gear repairs needed, things to bring next time:

....

....

....

....

....

....

140

LONG-TERM CAMPING TRIP 2

DATES: from [ ][ ][ ] to [ ][ ][ ]

Location

Attending

1

2

3

4

5

6

7

8

Things to do differently

Gear repairs needed, things to bring next time:

LONG-TERM CAMPING TRIP 3

DATES: from ☐☐☐ to ☐☐☐

Location

Attending

1

2

3

4

5

6

7

8

Things to do differently

Gear repairs needed, things to bring next time:

170

GENERAL PATROL NOTES

TITLE

TITLE

TITLE

NOTES

TITLE

TITLE

NOTES

TITLE

NOTES

TITLE

NOTES

NOTES

TITLE

NOTES

TITLE

NOTES

TITLE

NOTES

TITLE

216

Title

NAME

217

Title

NAME

Title

NAME

Title

								NAME

Title

NAME

221

Title

NAME

Title

NAME

223

Title

NAME

Title

NAME

225

Title

NAME

Title

NAME

Title

NAME

Title

NAME

Title

NAME

Title

NAME

231

Title

NAME

Title

NAME

233

Title

NAME

42376114R00137

Made in the USA
Lexington, KY
18 June 2015